Published by Barbour Publishing, Inc., P. O. Box 719, Uhrichsville, Ohio 44683, www.barbourbooks.com

Member of the
Evangelical Christian
Publishers Association

Printed in the United States of America.
5 4 3 2 1

THE LORD IS MY SHEPHERD

Selected Psalms of Encouragement

DayMaker GREETING BOOKS

The LORD is my shepherd;
I shall not want.

PSALM 23:1

Introduction

For thousands of years, the Psalms have brought comfort and encouragement to those who love God. The inspired words of David and the other psalm writers resonate through the ages with the unchanging truth that God is, and that He loves His children.

The Psalms deal honestly with the trials and turmoil of life—but they also return time and again to God's faithfulness toward man. God is true, He is merciful, He is powerful, He is loving.

This little book features carefully-selected Psalms to draw your thoughts to the God Who made you, keeps you, and loves you. As you read, you'll be reminded that the Lord is good, the Lord is faithful, *The Lord Is My Shepherd*.

Psalm 23

The LORD is my shepherd;
    I shall not want.
He maketh me to lie down in green pastures:
    he leadeth me beside the still waters.
He restoreth my soul:
    he leadeth me in the paths of righteousness
    for his name's sake.
Yea, though I walk through
    the valley of the shadow of death,
    I will fear no evil:

for thou art with me;
   thy rod and thy staff they comfort me.
Thou preparest a table before me
   in the presence of mine enemies:
   thou anointest my head with oil;
   my cup runneth over.
Surely goodness and mercy shall follow me
   all the days of my life: and I will dwell in
   the house of the LORD for ever.

Psalm 3

Lord, how are they increased that trouble me!
  many are they that rise up against me.
Many there be which say of my soul,
  There is no help for him in God. Selah.
But thou, O LORD, art a shield for me;
  my glory, and the lifter up of mine head.
I cried unto the LORD with my voice,
  and he heard me out of his holy hill. Selah.
I laid me down and slept; I awaked;

for the LORD sustained me.
I will not be afraid of ten thousands of people,
    that have set themselves against me round about.
Arise, O LORD; save me, O my God:
    for thou hast smitten all mine enemies
    upon the cheek bone;
    thou hast broken the teeth of the ungodly.
Salvation belongeth unto the LORD:
    thy blessing is upon thy people. Selah.

from Psalm 16

Preserve me, O God:
   for in thee do I put my trust.
O my soul, thou hast said unto the LORD,
   Thou art my Lord:
   my goodness extendeth not to thee;
But to the saints that are in the earth,
   and to the excellent, in whom is all my delight.
Their sorrows shall be multiplied
   that hasten after another god:
   their drink offerings of blood will I not offer,
   nor take up their names into my lips.
The LORD is the portion of mine inheritance
   and of my cup: thou maintainest my lot.

The lines are fallen unto me in pleasant places;
   yea, I have a goodly heritage.
I will bless the LORD,
   who hath given me counsel:
   my reins also instruct me in the night seasons.
I have set the LORD always before me:
   because he is at my right hand,
I shall not be moved.
Therefore my heart is glad,
   and my glory rejoiceth:
   my flesh also shall rest in hope.

from Psalm 25

Unto thee, O LORD, do I lift up my soul.
O my God, I trust in thee:
   let me not be ashamed,
   let not mine enemies triumph over me.
Yea, let none that wait on thee be ashamed:
   let them be ashamed which transgress
   without cause.
Shew me thy ways, O LORD;
   teach me thy paths.
Lead me in thy truth, and teach me:
   for thou art the God of my salvation;
   on thee do I wait all the day.

Remember, O LORD,
   thy tender mercies and thy lovingkindnesses;
   for they have been ever of old.
Remember not the sins of my youth,
   nor my transgressions:
   according to thy mercy remember thou me
   for thy goodness' sake, O LORD.
Good and upright is the LORD:
   therefore will he teach sinners in the way.

from Psalm 28

Blessed be the LORD,
    because he hath heard the voice of
    my supplications.
The LORD is my strength and my shield;
    my heart trusted in him, and I am helped:
    therefore my heart greatly rejoiceth;
    and with my song will I praise him.
The LORD is their strength,
    and he is the saving strength of his anointed.
Save thy people, and bless thine inheritance:
    feed them also, and lift them up for ever.

from Psalm 30

O LORD my God, I cried unto thee,
   and thou hast healed me.
O LORD, thou hast brought up my soul
   from the grave: thou hast kept me alive,
   that I should not go down to the pit.
Sing unto the LORD, O ye saints of his,
   and give thanks at the remembrance of
   his holiness.
For his anger endureth but a moment;
   in his favour is life:
     weeping may endure for a night,
     but joy cometh in the morning.

from Psalm 34

The eyes of the LORD are upon the righteous,
  and his ears are open unto their cry.
The face of the LORD is against them
    that do evil,
    to cut off the remembrance of them
    from the earth.
The righteous cry, and the LORD heareth,
  and delivereth them out of all their troubles.

from Psalm 36

How excellent is thy lovingkindness, O God!
   therefore the children of men put their trust
   under the shadow of thy wings.
They shall be abundantly satisfied with the
   fatness of thy house;
    and thou shalt make them drink of the river
    of thy pleasures.
For with thee is the fountain of life:
   in thy light shall we see light.

from Psalm 37

Fret not thyself because of evildoers,
   neither be thou envious against the workers
   of iniquity.
For they shall soon be cut down like the grass,
   and wither as the green herb.
Trust in the LORD, and do good;
   so shalt thou dwell in the land,
   and verily thou shalt be fed.
Delight thyself also in the LORD:
   and he shall give thee the desires of thine heart.

from Psalm 40

I waited patiently for the LORD;
    and he inclined unto me, and heard my cry.
He brought me up also out of an horrible pit,
    out of the miry clay,
    and set my feet upon a rock,
    and established my goings.
And he hath put a new song in my mouth,
    even praise unto our God:
    many shall see it, and fear,
    and shall trust in the LORD.

from Psalm 46

God is our refuge and strength,
  a very present help in trouble.
Therefore will not we fear,
  though the earth be removed,
  and though the mountains be carried
  into the midst of the sea;
Though the waters thereof roar and be troubled,
  though the mountains shake with the
  swelling thereof.
  Selah.

from Psalm 57

Be merciful unto me, O God,
  be merciful unto me:
  for my soul trusteth in thee:
  yea, in the shadow of thy wings
  will I make my refuge,
  until these calamities be overpast.
I will cry unto God most high;
  unto God that performeth all things for me.
He shall send from heaven,
  and save me from the reproach of him
  that would swallow me up. Selah.
  God shall send forth his mercy and his truth.

from Psalm 61

Hear my cry, O God;
    attend unto my prayer.
From the end of the earth will I cry unto thee,
    when my heart is overwhelmed:
    lead me to the rock that is higher than I.
For thou hast been a shelter for me,
    and a strong tower from the enemy.

from Psalm 62

My soul, wait thou only upon God;
   for my expectation is from him.
He only is my rock and my salvation:
   he is my defence; I shall not be moved.
In God is my salvation and my glory:
   the rock of my strength,
   and my refuge, is in God.
Trust in him at all times;
   ye people, pour out your heart before him:
   God is a refuge for us. Selah.

Psalm 67

God be merciful unto us, and bless us;
   and cause his face to shine upon us; Selah.
That thy way may be known upon earth,
   thy saving health among all nations.
Let the people praise thee, O God;
   let all the people praise thee.
O let the nations be glad and sing for joy:
   for thou shalt judge the people righteously,
   and govern the nations upon earth. Selah.

Let the people praise thee, O God;
  let all the people praise thee.
Then shall the earth yield her increase;
  and God, even our own God, shall bless us.
God shall bless us;
  and all the ends of the earth shall fear him.

from Psalm 71

In thee, O LORD, do I put my trust:
  let me never be put to confusion.
Deliver me in thy righteousness,
  and cause me to escape:
  incline thine ear unto me, and save me.
Be thou my strong habitation,
  whereunto I may continually resort:
  thou hast given commandment to save me;
  for thou art my rock and my fortress.

from Psalm 86

For thou, Lord, art good, and ready to forgive;
  and plenteous in mercy unto all them
  that call upon thee.
Give ear, O LORD, unto my prayer;
  and attend to the voice of my supplications.
In the day of my trouble I will call upon thee:
  for thou wilt answer me.

from Psalm 89

I will sing of the mercies of the LORD forever;
    with my mouth will I make known
    thy faithfulness to all generations.
For I have said,
    Mercy shall be built up for ever;
    thy faithfulness shalt thou establish in
    the very heavens.
O LORD God of hosts,
    who is a strong LORD like unto thee?
    or to thy faithfulness round about thee?

from Psalm 91

He that dwelleth in the secret place of
    the most High shall abide under
    the shadow of the Almighty.
I will say of the LORD,
    He is my refuge and my fortress: my God;
    in him will I trust.
Surely he shall deliver thee from the snare
    of the fowler,
    and from the noisome pestilence.
He shall cover thee with his feathers,
    and under his wings shalt thou trust:
    his truth shall be thy shield and buckler.

from Psalm 98

O sing unto the LORD a new song;
 for he hath done marvellous things:
 his right hand, and his holy arm,
 hath gotten him the victory.
The LORD hath made known his salvation:
 his righteousness hath he openly shewed
 in the sight of the heathen.
He hath remembered his mercy and his truth
 toward the house of Israel:
 all the ends of the earth have seen
 the salvation of our God.

Psalm 100

Make a joyful noise unto the LORD, all ye lands.
Serve the LORD with gladness:
    come before his presence with singing.
Know ye that the LORD he is God:
    it is he that hath made us, and not we ourselves;
    we are his people, and the sheep of his pasture.
Enter into his gates with thanksgiving,
    and into his courts with praise:
    be thankful unto him, and bless his name.
For the LORD is good;
    his mercy is everlasting;
    and his truth endureth to all generations.

from Psalm 103

Bless the LORD, O my soul:
  and all that is within me, bless his holy name.
Bless the LORD, O my soul,
  and forget not all his benefits:
Who forgiveth all thine iniquities;
  who healeth all thy diseases;
Who redeemeth thy life from destruction;
  who crowneth thee with lovingkindness
  and tender mercies;
Who satisfieth thy mouth with good things;
  so that thy youth is renewed like the eagle's.

The LORD is merciful and gracious,
  slow to anger, and plenteous in mercy.
He will not always chide:
  neither will he keep his anger for ever.
He hath not dealt with us after our sins;
  nor rewarded us according to our iniquities.
For as the heaven is high above the earth,
  so great is his mercy toward them that fear him.
As far as the east is from the west,
  so far hath he removed our transgressions
  from us.

from Psalm 111

Praise ye the LORD.
  I will praise the LORD with my whole heart,
  in the assembly of the upright,
  and in the congregation.
The works of the LORD are great,
  sought out of all them that have pleasure therein.
His work is honourable and glorious:
  and his righteousness endureth for ever.
He hath made his wonderful works
  to be remembered:
  the LORD is gracious and full of compassion.

from Psalm 112

Praise ye the LORD.
  Blessed is the man that feareth the LORD,
  that delighteth greatly in his commandments.
His seed shall be mighty upon earth:
  the generation of the upright shall be blessed.
Wealth and riches shall be in his house:
  and his righteousness endureth for ever.
Unto the upright there ariseth light
  in the darkness:
  he is gracious, and full of compassion,
  and righteous.

from Psalm 116

I love the LORD,
  because he hath heard my voice
  and my supplications.
Because he hath inclined his ear unto me,
  therefore will I call upon him as long as I live.
The sorrows of death compassed me,
  and the pains of hell gat hold upon me:
  I found trouble and sorrow.
Then called I upon the name of the LORD;
  O LORD, I beseech thee, deliver my soul.

Gracious is the LORD, and righteous;
  yea, our God is merciful.
The LORD preserveth the simple:
  I was brought low, and he helped me.
Return unto thy rest, O my soul;
  for the LORD hath dealt bountifully with thee.
For thou hast delivered my soul from death,
  mine eyes from tears, and my feet from falling.

from Psalm 118

Let them now that fear the LORD say,
   that his mercy endureth for ever.
I called upon the LORD in distress:
   the LORD answered me,
   and set me in a large place.
The LORD is on my side; I will not fear:
   what can man do unto me?

from Psalm 119

Thy righteousness is an everlasting righteousness,
  and thy law is the truth.
Trouble and anguish have taken hold on me:
  yet thy commandments are my delights.
The righteousness of thy testimonies is everlasting:
  give me understanding, and I shall live.

from Psalm 145

The LORD is righteous in all his ways,
  and holy in all his works.
The LORD is nigh unto all them that
  call upon him,
    to all that call upon him in truth.
He will fulfil the desire of them that fear him:
  he also will hear their cry,
    and will save them.